THE MIRACLE SQUAD

Libretto by
PAT BELFORD

by

SCENE 1 *HEAVEN, with Gabriel and the angels*

1. The Miracle Squad

© Oxford University Press 1988   Printed in Great Britain

OXFORD UNIVERSITY PRESS, MUSIC DEPARTMENT, GREAT CLARENDON STREET, OXFORD OX2 6DP
Photocopying this copyright material is **ILLEGAL**

Angel 1	Look, there's Mary. Shall we tell her?
Gabriel	Tell her what?
Angel 1	Shall we tell her that she's going to have a baby?
Gabriel	I was thinking of telling her tomorrow.
Angel 1	That's typical, Gabriel. You're always putting things off until tomorrow. Now's your chance. She's sitting in her house, all alone.
Angel 3	Just the right time to tell her.
Gabriel	Not just yet. I haven't quite decided what to say. I need to think about it.
Angel 4	*(jumping up eagerly)* How about 'Hi, Mary! Guess what? We've got the most tremendous news for you!'
Angel 2	That won't do. It must be dignified. And we mustn't frighten Mary. This is a special occasion.
Angel 3	Besides, that chap Luke is writing it all down for his gospel.
Angel 1	Well – are you going?
Gabriel	Wouldn't tomorrow do instead? I'd rather stay here just now. There's a good game between Jerusalem and Jericho starting down there. I'd like to watch it.
Angel 1	It's time you stopped sitting around and watching and did something useful.
Gabriel	All right. I'll go.*(mutters)* Nag, nag, nag. *(gets up)*
Angel 2	Get properly dressed first. Has his halo come back from the cleaners?
Angel 3	Yes, it's here.
	He gives it a quick polish.
Gabriel	I don't suppose there'll be any peace here in heaven until I go.
Angel 1	That reminds me. Don't forget to say 'Peace on earth' when you get there. 'Peace on earth, good-will to all men.' The people expect it.
Angel 4	*(looking admiringly at Gabriel)* Don't let Angel 1 upset you. She means well.
Gabriel	Right. I'm going down to tell Mary.

2. Don't Worry About A Thing

SCENE 2   HEAVEN, with Gabriel

Enter Angels 2 and 3 singing 'Glory to God in the Highest'. They carry song books.

Gabriel	Ah! Just the folk I wanted to see.
Angel 2	Hello Gabriel. We're in a bit of a hurry I'm afraid.
Gabriel	Where are you off to?
Angel 3	Singing practice. Angel 1 has got a choir of angels together.
Angel 2	We need a multitude of heavenly hosts to sing at some big event that's taking place shortly.
Gabriel	Oh – you mean the royal birth. There's plenty of time for that. We won't need the angel choir for weeks yet. There's something much more important for you to do.
Angel 3	What's that?
Gabriel	Get down to Caesar's palace. We've got to get Mary and Joseph back to the city of David somehow. If you can persuade Caesar Augustus to sign a decree, our problem will be solved.
Angel 2	A decree?
Gabriel	Yes – you know the kind of thing. Everyone has to go back to the place where he was born, to register.
Angel 3	A kind of census?
Gabriel	Yes, a census.
Angel 2	How are we going to persuade Caesar to do that? He's an awkward customer, you know. And I've heard that he takes all the taxes for himself.
Gabriel	Tell him that if he holds a census he'll be able to collect even more money from the people. That should do the trick.

Angels 2 and 3 put down their song books

Angel 2   Leave it to us! Come on, Three. Cheerio, Gabriel. We'll disguise ourselves as tax collectors.

Exit

SCENE 3   *CAESAR'S PALACE*

Enter Caesar, Angels 2 and 3, and Ministers

Caesar	What is your business in my palace?
Angel 2	I'm your new tax collector, sir. I'm replacing the old one. I'm the relief.
Caesar	Tax relief, eh? What happened to my other tax man?
Angel 3	Er – I think he's ill, sir. Yes – ill. He hopes to be back at work next week.
Caesar	These young people – they take time off whenever they feel like it. Well – what did you want to see me about?
Angel 2	I thought, sir, that it was time to collect more taxes from the people.
Caesar	Ah, increase taxation. Good man!
Angel 2	Yes, sir. In fact I've worked out a plan.
Angel 3	We've both worked out a plan. A new tax system.
Angel 2	We thought that if everyone went back to the town of his birth, he could be registered.
Angel 3	Then you could not only have a census and count everybody, but also decide how much tax money to collect from each man.
Caesar	Yes – I like that idea.
Angel 2	You were saying only the other day that you'd like to know how many people you have in your empire.
Caesar	So I did. But how do you know I said that? I've never seen you until today.

The angels look at each other

Angel 3	Ah, your majesty, we like to keep an eye on current events.
Caesar	Excellent! Most young people these days seem to have their heads in the clouds.
Angel 2	Oh, we have our heads in the clouds most of the time, sir, *(receives a kick from Angel 3)* – but never miss anything important.
Caesar	And the most important thing in the world is money – my money!

3. Pay Up!

SCENE 4   *HEAVEN, with angels*

Gabriel	Everything is going well now. The emperor has decided to hold a census, so Mary and Joseph will have to go to Bethlehem.
Angel 1	Poor Mary! What a time to have to travel all that way. Still, we must be sure that the baby will be born in Bethlehem as the prophets said.
Gabriel	And now — we must find three great kings.
Angel 2	The three kings? What are they going to do?
Gabriel	They will come from the east and worship the baby and bring presents for him. You two, *(turning to Angels 3 and 4)* get down there and go on a journey with the kings. Disguise yourselves as servants and see that they travel across the desert and reach Bethlehem safely.
Angel 3	The desert? People get lost in the desert.
Angel 4	How can we find the way?
Gabriel	The kings are studying their books now. Look — there they are! They're looking for a sign — a bright star in the east. Go with them — just follow the star.

Exit Angels 3 and 4. The other angels rise.

Angel 5	Can we do something?
Angel 6	Let us help too!
Angel 7	Yes, give us a job, please, Gabriel.
Gabriel	Very well. Go and find the brightest star and move it across the desert so that the three kings can follow it.
Angel 5	The brightest star!
Angel 6	We'll find it!
Angel 7	Just leave it to us!

Exit the three angels

Gabriel	*(calling into the wings)* Have you found it?
Angels	Yes! We've got it!
Gabriel	Good! Keep it up! Keep that star moving so that it guides the three kings.

4. Keep That Star A-Moving

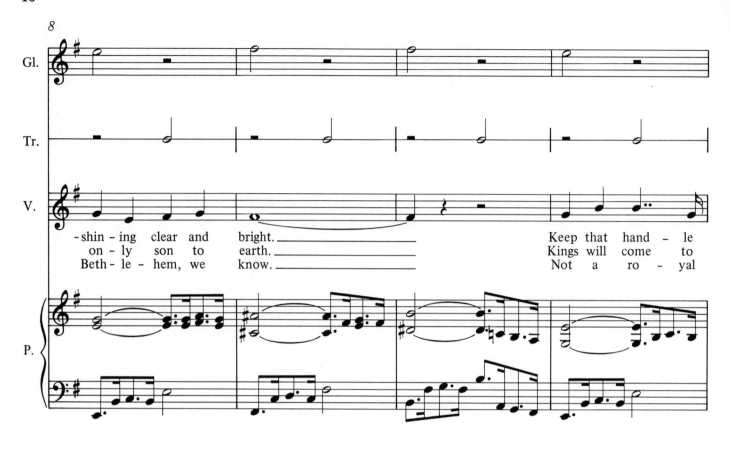

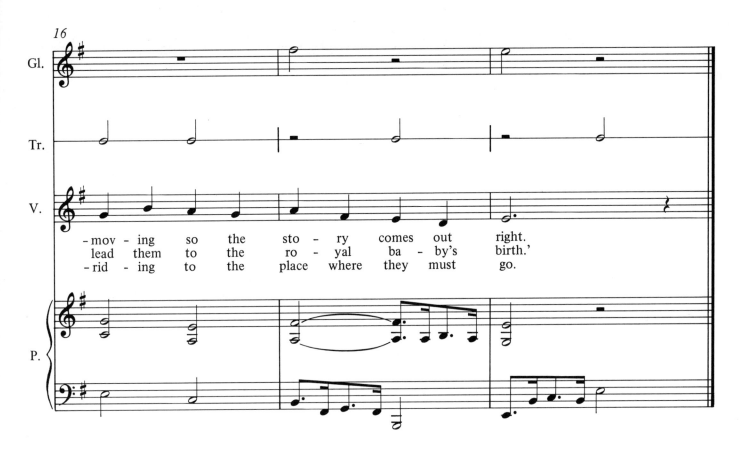

SCENE 5   HEAVEN   *Gabriel is seated with feet up, reading a newspaper.*

Enter Angels 1 and 2

Angels	Gabriel! Gabriel! Something terrible has happened!
Gabriel	*(still reading)* What now?
Angel 1	Those stupid angels have managed to get the star stuck in the wrong place!
Gabriel	*(lazily)* Well — tell them to move it!
Angel 2	They can't — it's too late! Oh why did you trust those three with such an important job?
Gabriel	Everyone makes mistakes!
Angel 1	But this is a disastrous mistake! They've put the star over Jerusalem and it's led the three kings to — to — to —
Gabriel	*(alarmed)* Where? Where?
Angel 1	To King Herod's palace!
Gabriel	What? Oh no! We must get them away quickly before King Herod sees them!
Angel 2	*(gazing down)* It's too late. They've gone into the palace. Look! they're talking to Herod!
Gabriel	They're asking him 'Where is the new baby king? Where is the King of the Jews?'
Angel 1	Quick! We must do something! You're the only one who can get us out of this mess. It's up to you Gabriel!

Exit Gabriel

5. The Star Stood Still

SCENE 6   *HEAVEN, several hours later*

Enter Angels 1 and 2

Angel 2	Oh I do hope Gabriel will be able to sort things out.
Angel 1	It's terrible, a disaster. I wish we could help.
Angel 2	Gosh! Gabriel must have fixed it! Look! The kings are moving on!

Enter Angel 3

Others	What happened?
Angel 3	Gabriel has sorted everything out. It was a great idea of his to send a dream.
Angel 1	A dream?
Angel 3	Yes. He warned the kings in a dream not to tell King Herod when the baby has been born. They're to go back home to the east by a different route after they've seen the baby.
Angel 2	Thank goodness! So our problems are over.
Gabriel	*(entering)* Not quite. There's more work to be done. Now we've got to go to Bethlehem.

SCENE 7   *BETHLEHEM, outside the Inn*

Angels 1 and 2

Angel 2	You *are* sure this is the right inn?
Angel 1	Yes. We must get everything right this time.
Gabriel	*(entering)* Ah, there you are! Where's the star?

Angels 5, 6, and 7 enter in haste and hold the star over the inn.

Gabriel	That's better. No mistakes tonight. *(to Angels 1 and 2)* Stay here and wait for Mary and Joseph. They're on their way to Bethlehem and your job is to make sure that they stay the night in this inn. Whatever happens they must stay here. This is where the royal birth will take place.
Angels	Leave it to us, Gabriel.

Exit Gabriel

Angel 1	There's someone coming now. Perhaps its Mary and Joseph.

Through the audience a blind man enters led by Paul and Sarah. Following closely is a maimed person on a litter carried by several people.

Angel 2	They don't look like Mary and Joseph, but they may have seen them.
Blind Man	Are we nearly there? I can't walk much further.
Paul	Just a few more steps, dad.
Angel 1	May we join you?
Sarah	Certainly. We're hoping to find an inn.
Angel 2	We know of a good one. It isn't far. This way.
Angel 1	Have you seen anyone else travelling on this road?
Paul	There's a young couple from Nazareth not far behind, but they're travelling more slowly and they turned off at the corner.
Angel 2	Here we are. We've arrived. This is the inn we told you about.

Approaches and knocks

Enter Innkeeper

Innkeeper	Good evening to you all. *(calls back inside to his wife)* More travellers!
Paul	Good evening. Have you a room for us, please?
Blind Man	We've walked a long way since morning.
Innkeeper	I can see that. Come in. You're all very welcome.
Wife	*(entering)* Yes. Come in and rest. We've plenty of food ready. *(to litter bearers)* You must be dead beat, carrying him all that way.
Man carrying litter	
	Well, everyone has to register, even the blind man and the maimed. There's no way out of it. We all have to obey the orders of the emperor.

Enters the inn with the others

Angel 1	*(to Angel 2, aside)* It looks as though we've missed Mary and Joseph.
Angel 2	No – look! They're coming now. There must be room for them in the inn.

Enter Mary and Joseph. They knock. The Inkeeper and his wife come to the door

Joseph	Good evening, landlord. Have you a room for the night?
Innkeeper	You're too late, I'm afraid. Only five minutes ago I took in a large group.
Wife	I expect you'll get a room somewhere else. There's quite a nice little place down the road.
Joseph	We've been there. It's full. All the inns in Bethlehem are full.
Wife	Aye, everyone's come for the census. I've never known Bethlehem so busy.
Joseph	We've nowhere to stay.
Mary	You're our last hope.
Angel 1	*(urgently)* Couldn't you fit them in somewhere?
Angel 2	In the stable, perhaps. They look very tired.
Innkeeper	Well, there's certainly room in the stable. And it is warm and dry. If you don't mind being in with the animals?
Mary	Oh, thank you.
Joseph	We don't mind the animals. Yes, we'll sleep in the stable.
Mary	Just as long as we can rest.
Angel 2	You'll bring some food for them, won't you?
Wife	Of course we will. There's plenty of food. We'll see to it at once.

Exit Wife

Angel 1	We'll leave you then. I hope you have a comfortable night. Good-night.
Joseph	Thank you, thank you for your help.
Mary	Good-night.

Exit Mary and Joseph

Angels	Good-night.

They stand outside for a moment and look skywards.

Angel 1	All's well, Gabriel.
Angel 2	*(to small angels)* Keep that star right there over the stable.
Gabriel	*(entering)* The baby is about to be born. Nothing else can go wrong now, thank goodness. You two, keep an eye on things here, and you three, *(to small angels)* don't move that star. Keep it right there so that the shepherds and kings can find the baby.

6. March Of The Kings

This music may be used for a Procession of the Kings.
If possible choose instruments with different tone-colours to make a difference between Bands 1 and 2 (for example by using tenor recorders in Band 2).

24

7. Thank Goodness

Gabriel   Now you must go and sing to the shepherds.
Angel 1   One more practice first, please.

8. Glory To God In The Highest

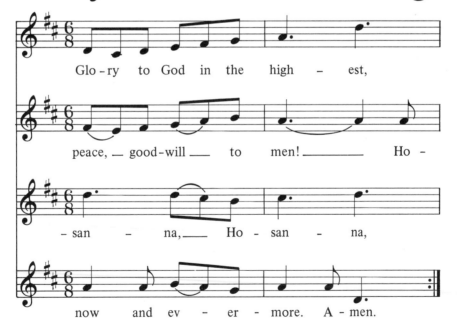

Angel 1   That's not loud enough. We need more people.
Gabriel   *(to audience)* You'll sing, won't you?

*The audience joins in, whilst some angels exit to fetch the shepherds.
Shepherds enter and the singing continues.
The kings follow.*

Gabriel   We've done what we set out to do. The baby king has been born. Peace on earth, good-will to all men.

9. The Miracle Squad
reprise